David Bowen's

ENGLISH IDIOM

2
HEART AND SOUL

Heart and Soul

Exploring the English Idiom - Part Two

Introduction

We speak from the body in so many ways::- in the first place, physically, to show or perhaps try to disguise our feelings but, just as often, idiomatically. The 'arm and the leg' is the frightful cost of something. If we need it we must 'pay through the nose'. We get a person 'off our back' if no longer a burden. We 'lose face' if our reputation falls or we may try to 'save face'.

In this second book on the English idiom you will find as many such examples as you will meet in a month, or a year. Who knows?!

David Bowen

CONTENTS

Care of the body

Body

Body and soul
      one 's entire self

Body clock
      the biological clock

Body language
      communication by gesture

Enough to keep body and soul together
      minimum earnings

Over my dead body
      totally without my consent

Arm

Chance your arm?

An arm and a leg
      a lot of money

As long as your arm
      much longer than that

At arm's length
      sufficiently detached to avoid contact

Chance you arm
      make an attempt, 'have a go'.

Give one's right arm
      whatever is needed for granting one's wish

Long arm of the law
      its far-reaching power

Make, or give, a long arm
      give help to reach something

Right arm
      capable assistant

Shot in the arm
    much needed fillip of encouragement

Twist the arm
    co-erce

Up in arms
    protesting

With open arms
    welcoming gladly

Within arm's reach
    near; close, as required

Put your back into it

Back against the wall
    in a desperate situation

Back-bite
    speak ill of another

Back-breaker
    hard, heavy job

Back-scratching
    giving favours for favours received

Get a person's back up
    irritate

Get off someone's back
    stop pestering

Put one's back into it
    perform a task vigorously

Stab someone in the back
    be disloyal

To the backbone
    through and through

Turn one's back on something
    abandon

Other backs

Answer back
    dispute what was said

(On the) back burner
    any relegated task or tasks

Back down
    abandon one's course to the will of another

Back number
    person with out-of-date ideas; old magazine, etc

Back o' beyond
    distant countryside

Back pedal
    reverse one's ideas or support

Back-room boy
    person doing possibly secret work in a special place

Back-slider
> one who goes back on his faith or ideals

Back stairs
> servants' quarters

Back to nature
> follow the course of a simple life-style

Back up (back-up, *noun*)
> support

Backward and forward
> to and fro

Break the back of
> finish the first part of the task

Get one's own back
> mild retaliation

Glad to see the back of something
> glad it is finished

Know something backwards
> be accomplished in a particular sphere

Lean over backwards
> go out of one's way to oblige another

See the back of
> be finished with a person or task

Take a back seat
> leave the main work to another

Through the back door
  through a clandestine arrangement

Blood

After someone's blood
  seeking explanation or perhaps revenge

Bad blood
  ill feeling towards another

Blood and thunder
  melodrama

Blood-curdling
  horrifying, especially in relation to drama

Blood is thicker than water
  family relationships take precedence

Blood money
  paid to a relative of one killed

Blood-sucker
  extortionate personality

Bloody-minded
  obstinate person

Blue blood
  member of the aristocracy, or royalty

In hot or cold blood
  with or without human passion

In one's blood
> inherited in one's character

Like getting blood out of a stone
> difficulty in obtaining something

Make one's blood boil
> infuriate

Make one's blood run cold
> horrify

New blood
> new intake of personnel

Out for someone's blood
> seeking retaliation

Sweat blood
> work very hard

Taste blood
> stimulation of conquest

Young blood
> new member, apprentice; new ideas

A bone to pick?

A bone of contention
> dispute

As dry as a bone
> dry and boring

A bone to pick
> a complaint to make

Bare bones
> the essential matter

Bone dry
> completely dry

Bonehead
> blockhead; stupid person

Bone idle
> completely idle

Boneshaker
> uncomfortable old vehicle

Bone up on
> study, collect information

Bone-weary
> exhausted

Bred in the bone
> a part of one's make-up

Close to the bone
> near indecent expression (also *near to the bone*)

Feel it in one's bones
> perceive through one's insight

Funny bone
> the humerus, close to the elbow

Have a bone in the throat
        cannot answer the question

Lazybones
        lazy person

Make no bones about it
        feel no scruples about some matter

Never make old bones
        unlikely to reach old age

Pick the bones out of
        grasp the essentials

Put flesh on the bones
        build up the picture

To the bone
        to the innermost

Work one's fingers to the bone
        work until exhausted

Got it on the brain?

Beat one's brains
        think very hard, puzzle intensively

Brainchild
        original idea

Brain drain
        loss of experts to another country

Brainfag
>> extreme mental tiredness

Brainstorm (*U.S.*)
>> thrash out a problem

Brainwash
>> systematically indoctrinate

Brainwave
>> sudden bright idea

Brainy
>> clever, intellectually outstanding

On the brain
>> what won't go away

Pick someone's brains
>> tap the knowledge of another

Plenty on top
>> a good brain

Rack one's brains
>> think hard

Make a clean breast

Make a clean breast of
>> make a full confession

Set the breast against
>> push forward, surmount

Strike one's breast
>> make a declaration

With the breast against
>> oppose

Breathtaking!

Breath of fresh air
>> any pleasant new experience

Breath of life
>> whatever necessity for that purpose

Breathe again
>> continue, following an interruption; recover after a shock

Breathe down a person's neck
>> close supervision of another person

Breathe easily
>> relief following a period of strain

Breather
>> short period of relaxation

Breathing space
>> a break, a brief respite

Breathtaking
>> astounding, amazing

Catch one's breath
>> recover one's breath

Draw breath
find a moment to relax

Hold one's breath
await something imminent

In the same breath
at the same time

Not breathe a word
keep quiet, keep a secret

Out of breath
panting from exertion

Save one's breath
refrain from pointless talk

Take a breath
stop for a break

Take a deep breath
prepare for a shock or disappointment

Take someone's breath away
astound, astonish

Under one's breath
in a low voice

Waste one's breath
fail to persuade, talk to no purpose

With bated breath
barely breathing, due to suspense

Browbeat?

Browbeat
       intimidate with stern looks

By the sweat of one's brow
       by one's own hard work

High, middle or low-brow
       intellectual level

Knit one's brow
       think about something

Troubled brow
       distressed, puzzled

Cheek of it!

'Blimmin' cheek'
       totally presumptuous, out of order

Cheek-by-jowl
       side by side, close proximity

Cheeky
>impertinent, impudent

Cheeky chappie
>comedian

None of your cheek!
>don't be impertinent!

The cheek of it!
>what impertinence!

Tongue in cheek
>words not to be taken too seriously

Turn the other cheek
>accept impertinence

Close to the chest

Get it off one's chest
>say what is in the mind

Lay it close to the chest
>be cautious, reveal no more than necessary

Chin up!

Chin-chin
>good-bye

Chinless wonder
>(*derog .*) receding chin

Chin-up!
    remain cheerful, especially when facing adversity

Chinwag
    informal talk, chat, gossip (*tsmiis, Filipino*)

Keep one's chin up
    (or *pecker up*) stay cheerful, despite problems

Take it on the chin
    accept adversity cheerfully

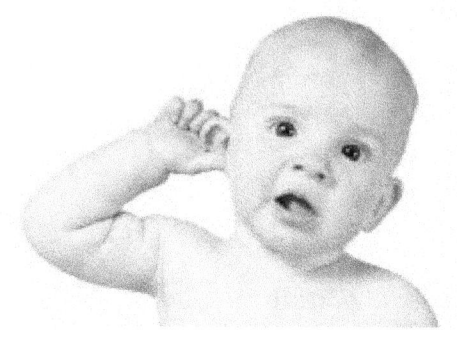

Earful

Ear

All ears
        paying great attention; eavesdropping

A word in one's ear
        private talk

Bring about one's ears
        bring trouble on oneself

Can't believe one's ears
        astounded

Cheerful little earful
        ironic a sharp talk of some kind

Earful
        a lot of what one would prefer not to hear

Ears burning
        someone is talking about you

Fall about one's ears
     fall all around

Flea in the ear
     angry

Have one's ear
     be sure of favourable attention

Have one's ear to the ground
     alert for information

In one ear and out the other
     bored with what is being said; paying no attention

Listen to reason
     be persuaded to act sensibly

Make a pig's ear
     make a mess of something

Make someone's ears warm
     speak of someone in his presence

Music to the ears
     very gratifying

Now I've heard it all!
     don't say any more!

Out on one's ear
     dismissed, humiliated

Prick up one's ears
     listen

Pin back someone's ear
   reprimand

Play it by ear
   improvise, as a situation develops

Set by the ears
   set against each other

Sympathetic ear
   welcome attention

Thick ear
   damage caused by a blow

Thrown out on one's ears
   hastily ejected

Turn a deaf ear
   purposely ignore

Up to one's ears
   deeply involved, very busy

Walls have ears
   unsafe to talk openly

Wet behind the ears
   naïve, immature

Saying There are none so deaf as those that do not want to hear

Elbow room

Bend (or crack) the elbow
      drink alcohol

Elbow grease
      humorous term for hard work

Elbow room
      plenty of space

Give the elbow
      eject a person

More power to someone's elbow
      give passive support

Out at the elbow
      generally ragged state of clothing

Rub elbows with
      meet important people

Eyesight

All eyes

All eyes
>very attentive

All my eye
>nonsense

Apple of one's eye
>endearing, very special person

Before your very eyes
>you have to believe it

Blind spot
>where lacking in judgement

Blue-eyed boy
>favoured person

Boss-eyed
>cross-eyed

Bright-eyed and bushy-tailed
> fresh appearance; on top form

Clap eyes on
> catch sight of

Close one's eyes to something
> an explanation, purposefully ignore

Cock an eye
> a glancing look

Cock-eyed
> out of true; nonsensical

Daylights
> the eyes

Dewy-eyed
> fresh, innocent

Do in the eye
> defraud

Dying to see
> anxious to do so

Eagle-eyed
> far-sighted

Easy as winking
> very simple

Evil eye
> superstitiously regarded as imparting harm

Eyeball to eyeball
>close contact in a frank discussion

Eye for an eye
>retaliation (*Exodus 21, 24*)

Eye-opener
>revelation

Eyes on beanstalks
>look of amazement

Eyesore
>offensive ugly building

Eyes peeled, or skinned
>on the watch-out for

Eye up
>ogle

Forty winks
>brief period of sleep

Give an eye to
>attend to

Give the glad eye
>amorous glance

Goggle-eyed
>stunned

Green in the eye
>gullible

Have an eye for
> be on the look-out for

Hit a person in the eye
> be very conspicuous, startle

In the mind's eye
> in imagination

In the twinkling of an eye
> very briefly

Keep a beady eye on
> watch carefully

Keep a weather eye open
> be on the look out

Light of one's eye
> much-loved person

Make sheep's eyes
> look flirtatiously

'Mud in your eye'
> informal toast

Not able to take one's eyes off
> total fixation

Not bat an eye-lid
> keep a straight face

One-eyed
> unpleasant place

One in the eye for
      rebuke, rebuff

Open a person's eyes
      enlighten

Private eye
      private detective

Pull the wool over someone's eyes
      fool, conceal

Raise an eyebrow
      look mildly reproving

See eye to eye
      be in agreement

See with half an eye
      without difficulty

Sight for sore eyes
      lovely to look at

Slap, lay or set one's eyes on
      be suddenly alert to something

Skew-eyed
      squinting; distorted

Smack in the eye
      rebuke

Smile in one's father's eye
      oneself before birth

Throw dust in the eye
     deceive

Tip the wink
     give a signal

Turn a blind eye
     deliberately not see

Up to the eyes
     extremely busy, deeply involved

With an eye to
     considering

With one eye shut
     do it easily

With one's eyes shut
     totally familiar task

Face to face

Face it

At face value
    at the normally stated value

Black in the face
    through temper or excessive effort

Brave face
    stoical

Cut off one's noise to spite one's face
    damage oneself in order to correct another

Face-ache
    facetious insult

Faceless
    lacking identity; some person with inferior judgement

Face the music
    accept unpleasant consequences

Face up to
> recognise the consequences of a challenge

Face someone down
> assert one's will by looking stern

Face up to
> recognise the consequences of a challenge

Forget one's own face
> admit forgetfulness

Fly in the face of
> set directly against

Get egg on one's face
> make a wrong judgement

Give someone or something a face lift
> carry out improvements

Grind the face of some-one
> govern some-one cruelly

Have a face like a fiddle or a long face
> never look cheerful or happy

Have the face to
> be brave enough, shameless enough

His or her face fell
> look suddenly disappointed

In the face of
> despite; as it appears

Laugh on he other side of one's face
    finish up far from laughing

Let's face it
    one must be realistic

Lose face
    lose prestige

On the face of it
    as it appears

Po-faced
    haughty

Pull a face
    grimace

Pull a long face
    look dismal

Put a brave face on it
    accept cheerfully

Put a good face on it
    make it look well

Put one's face on
    apply make-up

Puts a new face on
    alters the aspect altogether

Save one's face
    avoid humiliation

Set one's face against
        appear with determination

Show a face
        make an appearance

Slap in the face
        rebuff

Staring one in the face
        what is there all the time

To one's face
        in one's presence

Two-faced
        duplicitous, not to be trusted

When one's face falls
        look suddenly disappointed

Finger

A finger in the pie
        a share of the business

All fingers and thumbs
        fumbling

At one's finger-tips
        the relevant facts available

Burn one's fingers (*get one's fingers burnt*)
        invest unwisely

Butter- fingers
        cannot catch a ball

Cross one's fingers
        hopefully for good luck

Finger trouble (pull one's finger out)
        perform inefficiently

Have a finger in the pie
        an interest in some business or plan

Have green fingers
        skill with growing plants

Keep one's finger on the pulse
        maintain one's attention

Itchy fingers
        impatience with something to open, acquire

Keep one's finger on the pulse
        maintain one's attention

Lay a finger on
        cause harm to another; touch something one shouldn't

Let slip through one's fingers
        miss an opportunity

Light-fingered
        a thief

Not (won't) lift a finger
        fail to give help through laziness

Point the finger
> accuse, denounce

Put one's finger on something
> discover the relevant facts

Put the finger on
> inform against

Pull one's finger out
> get out and do something

Slip through the fingers
> miss an opportunity

Snap one's fingers
> sharp command

To one's finger-tips
> completely, precisely

Twist around the little finger
> dominate

What can be counted on one finger
> very little

Work one's fingers to the bone
> relentless hard work (*particularly domestic work*)

One's flesh

All flesh
>creatures, human and animal

A thorn in some-one's flesh
>an irritant

Flesh and blood
>the body (Saying, *More than flesh and blood can stand*
>more than be tolerated)

Flesh it out
>make substance

Fleshpot
>place of sexual entertainment

Get or have one's pound of flesh
>have all that one is entitled to

In the flesh
>in bodily form

Make the flesh creep
>frighten

Neither fish nor flesh
>difficult to decide what it is

One flesh
>the married state

Own flesh and blood
>family; descendants

Put flesh on the bones
     make substance

The spirit is willing but the flesh is weak
     lacking in stimulus

Way of all flesh
     common human experience

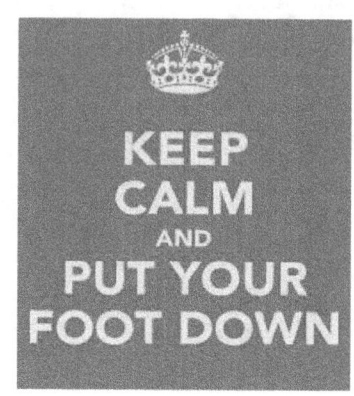

KEEP CALM AND PUT YOUR FOOT DOWN

Together?

Foot down?

At the feet of (*cast oneself at the feet of*)
> in submission

Best foot forward
> keep going, however tired

Boot in the door
> first step to success

Boot on the wrong or other foot
> no longer in control

Caught on the wrong foot
> unprepared

Cut the ground from under one's feet
> undermine

Drag one's feet
> be deliberately slow, or reluctant, to act

Feet of clay
>weakness of character

Follow in someone's footsteps
>do the same as the person one wishes to follow

Foot in the mouth
>verbal blunder

Foot-loose and fancy-free
>free to do as one wishes

Foot-slogging
>marching

Foot the bill
>pay up

Get cold feet
>change one's mind

Get off on the right or wrong foot
>make a good or a poor start

Fall on one's feet
>establish oneself

Find one's feet
>establish oneself; become accustomed to a situation

Get one's feet wet
>participate, start a job

Have both feet on the ground
>act with practical common sense

Have one's foot in the door
        prospect of success

Have the ball at one's feet
        be in control, have all within one's grasp

Have two left feet
        be clumsy and awkward, especially when dancing

Hoof it
        walk (back)

Hot-foot
        newly arrived

My foot!
        expression of disbelief

'My feet are killing me'
        ill-fitting shoes

Never put a foot wrong
        never blundered; never made a mistake

Not to put a foot wrong
        not to be in error

On a good footing
        having friendly contacts

On one's feet
        assured, determined

One foot in the grave
        very ill

Patter of tiny feet
     'new arrival'

Play footsie
     amorous movement of the foot, or leg

Put one's feet up
     take a rest

Put one's foot down
     decide firmly against the plan of another

Put one's foot in it
     make a blunder, indiscretion

Run off one's feet
     very busy

Set on foot
     originate; proceed with a plan

Set someone on his feet
     start in business

Shake the dust off one's feet
     not go there again

Shoot oneself in the foot
     harm one's own interests through incompetence

Stand on one's own two feet
     be independent

Steady on one's feet
     reliable

Swept off one's feet
       fall madly in love

Tread on someone's corns
       annoy a friend, disregard his feelings

With both feet on the ground
       practical common sense

Keep your hair?

Hair on

By a hair (or hair's breadth)
    by a very narrow margin

Get in a person's hair
    annoy, irritate

Hair-brained (also *hare-brained*)
    stupid

Hairdo
    set or style of a woman's hair

Hair of the dog
    a little more of what caused the trouble

Hair-raising
    frightening

Hair shirt
    austere, penitential garment

Hairy
>　risky

Keep your hair on!
>　don"t get angry!

Let one's hair down
>　abandon restraint

Make the hair stand on edge
>　terrify

Not turn a hair(or *without turning a hair*)
>　remain calm, unruffled

Split hairs
>　make fine distinctions, quibble

Tear one's hair out
>　act of extreme frustration

To a hair (or *to the turn of a hair*)
>　precisely

Touch your forelock
>　show of respect

Touch of the hands

Hands on

A hand (*nautical*)
> a sailor (as in *all hands on deck!*)

At first hand
> information direct from the source

At hand (close to hand)
> near, accessible

Back-hander
> bribe *or* ironic compliment

Bite the hand that feeds one
> offend a benefactor

Cack-handed (*slang*)
> clumsy

Catch red-handed
> catch a criminal in the act

Change hands
>   change of ownership

Charge-hand
>   foreman

Dab hand
>   especially skilled at something

Dead hand
>   stifling influence

Eat out of someone's hand
>   docile person

Even—handed
>   fair to all

Fire in the one hand, water in the other
>   say different things at different times

Force someone's hand
>   co-erce

Free hand
>   make one's own decision

Get one's hands on something or someone
>   acquire or detain

Get one's hand in
>   get accustomed to a task, some measure of control

Give a hand
>   give help, assist

Give one's hand
>in marriage

Golden handshake
>gift of money from employer

Good hand
>acceptable, reliable person

Ham-fisted
>heavy-handed, bungling

Handful
>person, usually a child, difficult to control

Hand -in-glove
>liaison with another for selfish purposes

Hand it out
>punish

Hand in velvet glove
>firm control despite gentle appearance

Hand it to someone
>acknowledge another's achievement

Hand-out
>contribution to a person in need

Hand over fist
>liberally

Hands-on approach
>taking a practical role

Hand something down
pass on a valuable object to another

Hand-to-mouth
living from day to day with nothing in reserve

Handy (*come in handy*)
useful, perhaps some article not required by another

Have a hand in
contribute to a project

Have one's hands tied
be too busy to take on further commitments

Heavy handed
clumsy; overbearing manner

Helping hand
much needed assistance

High-handed
arrogant manner

Hold, or stay, one's hand
wait before taking action or retaliation

In hand (or *well in hand*)
receiving attention

In the palm of one's hand
under one's control

Iron-fisted
tyrannical

Keep one's hand in
    continue the particular role

Know like the back of one's hand
    be very familiar with something

Lay hands on
    acquire; assault

Left hand not know what the right is doing
    be in a confused state

Lend a hand
    assist

Lift a hand (*normally used in the negative*)
    make an effort

Lily-white hands
    unworked

Live hand
    alert capable person

Lone hand
    lone worker

'Look, no hands!'
    conjuring trick

Make a good fist of something
    a good attempt, satisfactory job

Near or at hand (close at hand)
    readily available

Off-hand
> curt, ungracious and awkward manner; *or in the sense of speaking without preparation*

Off one's hands
> no longer one's responsibility

Old hand
> one already familiar with a particular role

On hand
> ready for use

On one's hands
> a commitment

One-handed
> single operation

Out of hand
> achievable without previous thought also unable to be controlled

Play into the hands of
> unintentionally give another the advantage

Poor hand
> unsatisfactory, unskilled person for the job

Second hand
> already used

Set one's hand to something
> undertake some mission or activity

Shake hands on something
  agree a deal

Show of hands
  assess agreement, or otherwise

Show one's hand
  expose one's purpose , intention

Sit on one's hands
  take no action

Stand one's hand
  buy drinks for another, or others

Strong hand
  decisive, reliable person

Take a person in hand
  control someone, correct his or her faults

Take clean out of one's hands
  lose control to another

Take in hand
  undertake some work; give firm treatment to a junior

Take one in hand
  become responsible, self sufficient

Take one's courage in both hands
  be brave

Take off someone's hands
  relieve someone of unwanted possessions or responsibility

Take someone's life in your hands
　　attempt something risky

Throw in one's hands
　　give up a venture

Tie someone's hands
　　prevent from acting independently

Tight-fisted
　　miserly, mean

To hand
　　in readiness

Try one's hand
　　attempt, experiment, 'give it a go'

Turn one's hand to
　　apply oneself to a task

Underhand
　　deception

Under one's hand
　　one's signature

Upper hand
　　mastery, the advantage

You've got to hand it to someone
　　acknowledge his or her contribution

Wait hand and foot upon
　　be subservient to another

Wash one's hands of
    disclaim responsibility

Whip hand
    whoever has control

Win hands down
    clear, easy win

Wring one's hands
    clasp one's hands in distress or puzzlement

Sayings

Many hands make light work

    that some might argue is contradicted by another,

Too many cooks spoil the broth.

Will they separate?

Head up

Above one's head
　　beyond one's understanding

A nod's as good as a wink
　　no need to say anything

Bang your head against a brick wall
　　try in vain to make a person understand

Be off one's head
　　be crazy, deranged

Bighead
　　conceited, pompous individual

Bite someone's head off
　　respond severely; angry outburst

Blockhead
　　stupid person

Blow one's top
> get angry

Bonehead
> (*as blockhead*)

Bring to a head
> bring to a climax

Bury one's head in the sand
> refuse to face the facts

By a short head
> by a narrow margin

Can't make head or tail of
> cannot understand

Come into one's head
> what occurs to one

Crack one's head
> knock one's head

Flip one's lid (*slang*)
> lose self control

Get it into one's head
> conceive the wrong idea

Get one's head down
> go to bed, take a rest

Give someone his head
> allow him to use his own initiative

Go out of one's head
    go crazy

Go over someone's head
    consult at a more senior level

Go to one's head
    be conceited, or slightly drunk

Hang one's head
    sad expression

Have a good head on one's shoulders
    have good judgement

Have a head for
    be good at something

Hard-headed
    shrewd in business, low in human sensitivity

Have one's head in the clouds
    dreaming about something

Have one's head screwed on the right way
    sensible, wise

Headache
    source of worry

Head and shoulders above
    vastly superior

Headbanger
    crazy person

Headful of bees
	strange notions

Head hunt
	search for a candidate for an important role

Head in the clouds
	in a dreamy state

Headlong
	rashly, without giving proper thought

Head off
	deflect, divert opposition

Head on
	close, probably a collision

Head over heels
	somersault

Head over heels in love
	in love to the exclusion of nearly everything else

Headshrinker (*slang)*
	psychiatrist

Heads will roll
	people will be disgraced or dismissed

Hit the headlines
	attract a lot of attention

Hold one's head up
	show self-confidence

Hold a pistol to one's head
> coerce

Hot-headed
> fiery temperament

Keep one's head
> stay calm

Keep one's head above water
> have sufficient income

Knock heads together
> insist on a sensible arrangement

Knock one's head against a wall
> face total opposition

Knock something on the head
> put an end to the problem

Lose one's head, rocker or trolley
> lose one's self control , act in a fit of madness

Make headway
> make progress

Need it like a hole in the head
> don't need it at all

Need one's head examined
> made a stupid mistake, thoughtless act

Out of one's head
> from memory, spontaneously

Need like a hole in the head
      not need at all

Nod through something (*process known as 'on the nod'*)
      obtain acceptance by nodding the head

Not make head or tail of it
      not understand

Not quite right in the head
      an odd kind of person or rebuke

Off or out of one's head
      crazy

Off the top of one's head
      impromptu thoughts

On one's head be it
      acceptance of responsibility

Over one's head
      beyond one's capacity to understand

Put heads together
      consult

Put one's head in a noose or on the block
      bring about one's own downfall

Rear its' ugly head
      come to believe wrongly

Soft in the head
      stupid

Take it into one's head
>> come to believe

Talk one's head off
>> never cease talking

Talk through the back of one's head
>> talk rubbish

Thickhead
>> stupid person

Turn a person's head
>> cause to become conceited

Two heads are better than one
>> better to work together

Wooden-headed
>> *same as 'blockhead'*

Big-hearted?

Heart

After one's own heart
       very much to one's own liking

At heart
       true feelings

Big-hearted
       generous

Break someone's heart
       cause deep sorrow

By heart
       repeated from memory

Change of heart
       change of mind and feelings; revoke a decision

Cross one's hart
       make the sign of the cross as a symbol of truth

Cry one's heart out
      give way to sorrow

Dear heart
      to one's heart

Dear to the heart
      a warm interest or concern

Do one's heart good
      be a pleasure

Don't take it to heart
      don't take it too seriously

Eat one's heart out
      brood over a mistake

Find it in one's heart
      bring oneself to do what is desired

From the bottom of one's heart
      fervently

Give someone heart
      moral support

Give someone heart failure
      give someone a bad shock

Hand on heart
      as a sign one is telling the truth

Have a heart!
      be reasonable!

Have a heart of gold
        kind, worthy person

Have at heart
        cherish

Have one's heart in it
        show enthusiasm

Have one's heart in one's boots
        depressed spirits

Have one's heart in one's mouth
        fearful

Have one's heart in the right place
        be decent, generous

Have one's heart set on
        earnestly desire something

Have the heart to
        resolution

Heartache
        sadness

Heart and soul
        with complete sincerity

Heart-breaker
        callous, fickle person

Heartfelt
        sincere

Heart of gold
>generous nature

Heart of hearts
>innermost feelings

Heart of oak
>brave, resolute

Heart-searching
>examining one's deepest feelings

Heart's ease
>peace of mind

Heart-stirring
>rousing, exhilarating

Heart-throb
>sentimental attachment of a member of the opposite sex

Heart to heart
>cordial discussion between two people

Heart-warming
>feeling of pleasure

In good heart
>in good condition (*of land*)

In one's heart of hearts
>one's deepest feelings

Lose heart
>become discontented

Lose one's heart to
      fall in love with

'My heart bleeds for you!'
      sour-natured retort

My heart goes out to somebody
      feel great pity

My heart sinks
      feel depressed

Not to have the heart to do something
      be reluctant to do it

One's heart is not in something
      not enthusiastic

Out of heart
      dispirited

Pour your heart out
      tell all

Put new heart into
      give encouragement

Put one's heart in it
      apply oneself with vigour

Set one's heart on
      desire very much

Set someone's heart at rest
      render ease of mind

Sick at heart
>> extremely disappointed

Speak from the heart
>> sincerely

Speak to the heart
>> encourage, comfort, reassure

Take heart
>> be encouraged

Take to heart
>> absorb for one's future guidance

Take to one's heart
>> the person who has claimed one's affection

To one's heart's content
>> as much as one needs

Tug of the heart strings
>> appeal to ones feelings

Warms the cockles of the heart
>> gladness

Wear one's heart on one's sleeve
>> make obvious one's feelings for another

With a heavy heart
>> sadly

With all one's heart (*with one's whole heart*)
>> totally committed

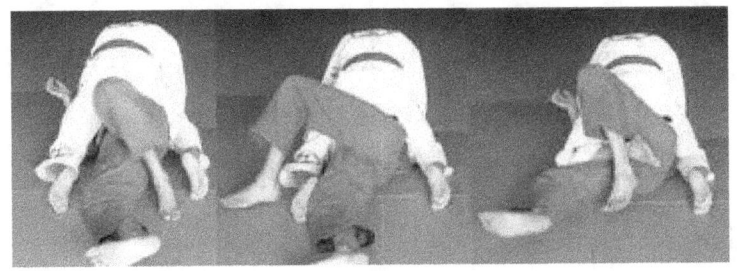

Drag the heel

Heels

An Achilles' heel
  a person's one weakness

Back on one's heels
  defensive attitude

Bring to heel
  to follow like a dog

Brisk pair of heels
  fast on one's feet

Clean pair of heels
  fast retreat

Come to heel
  conform

Cool or kick one's heels
  be kept waiting

Dig in one's heels
  resist, maintain a stubborn attitude

Down at heel
  in a poor state, shabbily dressed

Drag one's heels
  be deliberately slow to make a move

Head over heels
  upside-down

Hard on some-one's heels
  close behind

Lay by the heels
  fetter, confine

Pick up one's heels
  get moving, dance

Set one back on one's heels
  retard, disappoint

Show a clean pair of heels
  move fast

Take to one's heels
  run away

Tread on someone's heels
  come close behind

Under the heel
  oppressed

Walk to heel
  remain by the heels of another

Well-heeled
>   wealthy

Hip, hip

Hip-cat
>   jazz devotee

'Hip, hip ...'
>   give a cheer

Hip-huggers
>   trousers to fit on the hip, not the waist

Hippie (hippy)
>   1960's-style rebel against convention

Hipster
>   member of the beat generation

Shoot from the hip
>   talk bluntly

Jaw, jaw

Crack-jaw
>   words that are difficult to pronounce

Hold one's jaw
>   stop talking

Jaw
>   speak at great length

Jaw-breaker
　　　long word difficult to pronounce

Lantern jaws
　　　long thin jaws and chin

Sock on the jaw
　　　a punch

Saying Jaw -jaw is better than war-war (Winston Churchill)

Knees up

Knees

Bend the knee
    submit, venerate

Bring someone to his knees
    defeat

Knee-deep
    deeply immersed, involved

Knee-high to a grasshopper
    very short person

Knee-jerk reaction
    instant, without prior thought

Knees-up
    lively dancing of a party crowd

On one's bended knee
    in supplication, worship

Weak—kneed
    feeble, lacking resolution

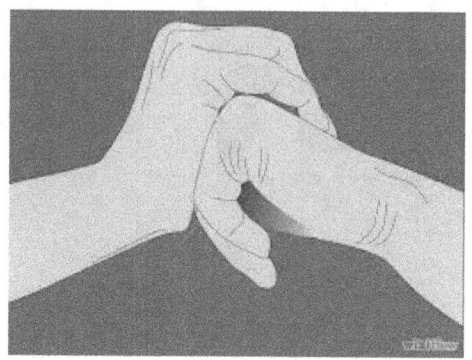

Knuckles

Flex the knuckles

Knuckle down
    set oneself to work

Knuckle under
    yield to pressure

Near the knuckle
    on the verge of indecency

Rap someone's knuckle
    reprimand

Lap

Drop into one's lap
    acquire fortuitously

In the lap of luxury
    luxurious conditions

In the lap of the gods
      result awaited

Lap of honour
      ceremonial circuit of a victor

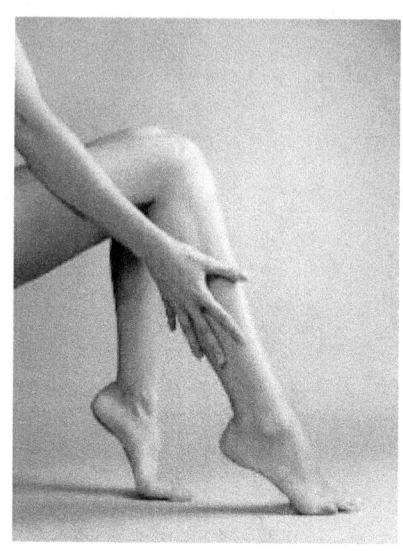

Feel one's leg

Leg

Feel (find) one's legs
  feel able to support oneself

Gammy leg
  not properly functioning

Give a leg up
  help someone through a difficulty

Have no legs
  somewhat drunk

Leggy
  long legs; showing the leg

Leg it
> walk

Leg warmers
> long socks

Leg-work
> walking or marching

Not a leg to stand on
> unable to explain or support an argument

On its last legs
> towards the end of its useful life

On one's last legs
> exhausted

Out on a limb
> on one's own, lacking support

Pull someone's leg
> a hoax,

Pull the other one (*leg*)
> I don"t believe you

Sea legs
> learning to balance oneself at sea

Set on one's legs
> made independent

Shake a leg!
> Hurry, get moving!

Show a leg
>> get out of bed

Stir one's stumps
>> move

Stretch one's legs
>> walk, after sitting

Tail between one's legs
>> downcast

Take to one's legs
>> get moving, escape

Lip

Bite one's lips
>> stifle one's retort

Give the lip
>> cheeky, insolent response

Hang on to a person's lips
>> listen attentively

Keep a stiff upper lip
>> show fortitude, resolve

Lick (or smack) one's lips
>> in pleasant anticipation

Lip-deep
>> insincere

Lippy
  insolent, cheeky

Lip service
  insincere

Make a lip
  pout

Many a slip between cup and lip
  last moment problems

My lips are sealed
  not willing to reveal

Not pass one's lips
  remain a secret

Pay lip service to something
  act as though in agreement

Liver

Lily-livered
  cowardly

Liverish
  disorderly state of one's liver and temper

Do you mind?

A load off one's mind
  mental relief

Absent-minded
        forgetful

At the back of one's mind
        vaguely remembered

Be of a mind
        set on a course of action

Bear (keep) in mind
        consider but not promise

Brings to mind
        suddenly occurs to one

Cast one's mind back
        recall an earlier event

Change one's mind
        decide otherwise

Close one's mind
        be unreceptive to fresh proposals

Cross one's mind
        sudden thought

Do you mind?
        Is it all right with you? (or as *protest, 'I don't like what you have just said or done'*)

Don't mind me!
        You are not considering me!

From time out of mind
        from the earliest time

Grasshopper mind
    making different decisions

Give someone a piece of one's mind
    a sharp rebuke

Great minds think alike
    clever people have the same ideas

Have a mind of one's own
    independence of thought

Have a one track mind
    cannot be diverted from a single issue

Have a (good) mind to
    am (seriously) considering

Have a person (or something) in mind
    am considering a suitable person (or whatever)

Have half a mind to
    I may well do this or that thing

Have in mind
    some particular intention

Have it in mind to
    take a particular course of action

Have on one's mind
    some worrying thought, problem or task

I don't mind
    I have no objection

I don't mind if I do
        I should rather like to do this

'If you don't mind'
        thank-you, with your consent

In the mind's eye
        in the imagination

In one's right mind
        sane

In one's mind's eye
        in one's thoughts

In the same mind
        in total accord

In two minds
        undecided

Keep an open mind
        willing to consider a proposal

Know one's own mind
        positive in thought and action

Little things please little minds
        our pleasures show the state of our minds

Make up one's mind
        decide

Mind-bending
        permanently inclining the mind to a particular belief

Mind-blowing
>confusing, overwhelming

Mind-boggling
>astounding

Mind how you go
>take care

'Mind one's own business'
>rebuke to the over-curious

Mind one's P's and Q's
>be careful of one's behaviour

'Mind out!'
>be careful, get out of the way

Mind over matter
>the mind is the more powerful

Mind the shop
>temporarily take charge

Mind type
>fair-minded, like minded, etc

Mind you
>an opinion to be taken into account

'Mind your back!'
>give way to something heavy

Never mind
>don't worry about it

Never you mind!
>your question is impertinent!

Not to know one's own mind
>not know how to think or do

Of the same mind
>in agreement

On one's mind
>perhaps a duty or problem, or an ongoing thought

Out of sight, out of mind
>temporarily forgotten

Out of one's mind
>crazy

Peace of mind
>a calm and settled mind

Presence of mind
>able to take calm decisions

Put one's mind at rest
>reassure

Put one's mind to
>focus

Put out of mind
>don't think about, ignore

Put some-one in mind of
>remind some-one of something

Put some-one's mind at rest
      free some-one of anxiety

Read a person's mind
      know his thoughts

Speak one's mind
      speak openly, frankly

Take somebody's mind off
      distract

Time out of mind
      from earliest time

To my mind
      in my opinion

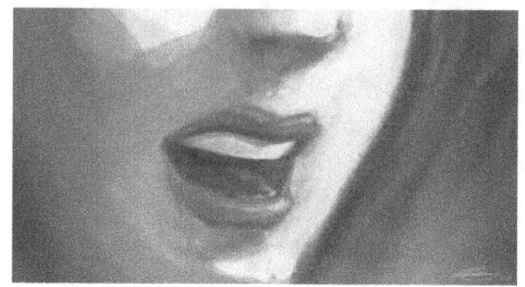

All mouth

Big mouth

A mouth, all mouth, big mouth
>   blabbermouth, boastful, talkative person

Butter wouldn't melt in his mouth
>   person with deceptively innocent manner

By word of mouth
>   as spoken, not written

Chew it over
>   think about it, consider it

Down in the mouth
>   unhappy, miserable

Extra mouth
>   another to feed

Gob (*slang*)
>   mouth

Gobsmacked (*slang*)
>   astounded

Hand to mouth
 enough for only immediate needs

Keep one's mouth shut
 keep a secret

Kisser (*slang*)
 the mouth

Leaves a nasty taste in the mouth
 unsatisfactory treatment

Mealy-mouthed
 smooth-tongued

Mouth-watering
 highly appetising

Mouthy
 bombastic, ranting

Put a sock in it!
 please be quiet

Put one's money where one's mouth is
 deeds count more than words

Shoot one's mouth off
 talk too much

Shut your trap! (*to a child*)
 stop talking!

Take the words out of a person's mouth
 say what was in another's mind

Muscle

Flex one's muscles
>show of strength, and readiness

Muscle in
>grab a share in another's enterprise

Not move a muscle
>stay motionless

Nails (*not only human*)

Bite one's nails
>from anxiety

Hard as nails
>callous, indifferent to others' problems

Hit the nail on the head
>express a point exactly

Nail a lie
>expose it

Nail in a person's coffin
>deed or occurrence supposed to increase the risk of death

Nail one's colours to the mast
>commit oneself to a plan of action

On the nail
>on the spot

What a neck!

Neck

Breakneck
    violent hurry

Breathe down a person's neck
    uncomfortably close, menacing

By the scruff of one's neck
    physically ejected

Daft from the neck up
    very stupid

Get it in the neck
    reprimand

Got a neck
    impudent

Have the neck to
    the audacity

Neck and crop
    the lot, completely, absolutely

Neck and neck
    running level in a race

Neckerchief
    scarf

Necking (*slang*)
    close embrace

Neck of the woods
    where one happens to live

Pain in the neck
    whoever makes himself a nuisance

Save one's neck
    escape

Stick one's neck into
    interfere with the affairs of another

Stick one's neck out
    take undue risks

Stiff-necked
    obstinate

Talk through the back of one's neck
    nonsensically

Turned out on one's neck
       dismissed, ejected

Up to one's neck
       too busy to tackle anything else

What a neck!
       what impudence!

Nose

A nose for something
       a talent for discovering

As plain as the nose on your face
       very obvious

By a nose
       by a small margin

Cut off one's nose to spite one's face
       injure oneself in an attempt to punish another

Follow one's nose
       go by instinct, take the obvious course

Get a bloody nose
       fare badly

Get up a person's nose
       irritate

Hard-nosed
       unbending

Keep one's nose clean
        stay out of trouble

Keep one's nose out (of)
        don't interfere

Keep one's nose to the grindstone
        keep laboriously working

Lead someone by the nose
        treat as a subordinate

Look down one's nose (at)
        despise

Nose in the air
        haughty

Nose job
        plastic surgery on the nose

Nose out of joint
        irritable

Nose to tail
        impacted traffic unable to move

Nosey (*Nosey Parker*)
        prying (*prying person*)

No skin off my nose
        of no consequence to me

Not see the end of one's nose
        short-sighted

Pay through the nose
      be charged a scandalously high price

Put a person's nose in it
      remind him of his earlier troubles

Put someone's nose out of joint
      irritate, embarrass, obstruct

Poke your nose into
      interfere in another's affairs

Rub someone's nose in it
      remind him of his past mistake

Look no further than the end of one's nose
      be unaware of the consequence

See beyond the end of one's nose
      see beyond current happenings

Sniffy
      disdainful

Thumb one's nose (*cock-a-snook*)
      make a disdainful sign

Toffee-nosed
      haughty, pretentious

Turn up one's nose
      act disdainfully

Under one's very nose
      openly, brazenly

Under one's nose
       in full view

With one's nose in the air
       haughty, superior attitude

Palm

In the palm of one's hand
       under one's control

Grease one's palm
       offer a bribe or incentive

Have an itching palm
       great desire for

Palm off
       inferior object or goods offered as perfect

Rib

A ribbing
       teasing

Rib-tickling
       very funny joke

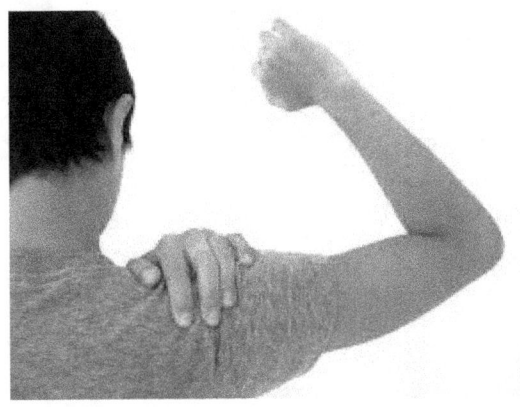

Touch on the shoulder

Shoulder

Chip on one's shoulder
     bear a grudge

Cold-shoulder
      indifference, reject another person

From the shoulder
     frankly

Have a good head on one's shoulders
     have good judgement

Have broad shoulders
      accept a great deal of responsibility

Head and shoulders above
     very much above

Look over your shoulder
     be distracted

Rub shoulders with
        meet accidentally

Set one's shoulder to the wheel
        begin the work

Shoulder of mutton
        triangular sail

Shoulder to cry on
        faithful companion

Shoulder to shoulder
        side by side, closed ranks

Straight from the shoulder
        frankly speaking

Shrug one's shoulders
        expose doubt, indecision

Too much on one's shoulders
        too many commitments

Skin

All skin and bone
        painfully thin

By the skin of one's teeth
        by a very narrow margin

Chance one's skin
        take a big risk

Change one's skin
  one's character

Jump out of one's skin
  get a fright

Get under one's skin
  annoy, irritate

No skin off one's nose
  matter of indifference

Skinned
  swindled, overcharged

Skinny
  thin

Save one's skin
  save oneself

Skin deep
  shallow display of affection

Skinful
  liberal amount of alcohol

Skinhead
  youth, probably gang member, with closely cropped hair

Skinny dip
  bathe naked

Skinny dipper
  tight-fitting sweater

Skin-tight
>> close-fitting

Thin or thick skinned
>> sensitive person or otherwise

Spine

Spine-chilling
>> fearful, frightening (*especially in drama*)

Spineless
>> lacking courage or substance

Stomach (Belly)

Bellyache
>> grumble (if not a pain in the stomach)

Belly-button
>> navel

Bellyflop
>> dive that falls flat on the water

Belly- landing
>> crash-landing by an aircraft

Bellyful
>> too much of whatever

Fight the flab
>> reduce one's weight

Flog one's guts out (*slang*)
>hard manual labour

Got guts
>courage

Gut rot (*slang*)
>cheap alcohol

Gutsy
>greedy (*or*) plucky

Gutted
>physically exhausted

Have a strong stomach
>to be able to deal with off-putting situations

Have no stomach for
>lack sufficient courage

Soft underbelly
>the vulnerable part of anything

Stomach something (or otherwise)
>endure, or otherwise

Turn some-one's stomach
>cause disgust in a person

Have a throat

Be at each others' throats
>in bitter argument

Cut one's own throat
      bring about one's own downfall

Cut-throat
      very competitive prices

Frog in the throat
      hoarseness

Give someone the lie in his throat
      make an accusation

Have a throat
      have a sore throat

Jump down someone's throat
      give an angry response

Lie in the throat
      lie outrageously

Lump in the throat
      sadness

Ram down someone's throat
      insist on one's strong belief

Stick in the throat
      feelings more than one can bear

Throaty
      sore throat

Too much to swallow
      what beggars belief

Thumb up

Thumbs

Be all thumbs
      clumsy

Rule of thumb
      roughly reckoning

Sticks out like a sore thumb
      very obvious

Thumb a lift
      beg a lift from a passing vehicle

Thumb one's nose (*cock a snook*)
      make a derisory sign

Thumbs up or down
      sign of approval, or disapproval

Thumb through
      quickly turn the pages

Twiddle the thumbs
    revolve them and do little else

Under some-one's thumb
    dominated

Well thumbed
    soiled pages of a book

Toe

On one's toes
    alert, eager

Take to one's toes
    turn away, escape

Toerag
    term of contempt for a vagrant, tramp

Toehold
    an initial (working) advantage

Toe the line
    conform to the rules laid down

Tread on someone's toes
    offend

Tongue

Bite one's tongue
    make an effort to remain silent

Double-tongued
insincere

Find, or lose, one's tongue
find, or lose, one's speech

Give tongue
speak one's thoughts

Hold your tongue (to a child)
keep quiet

Honey-tongued
persuasive

Keep a civil tongue in your head
avoid giving offence

Let one's tongue run away with one
speak too much when excited

Lose one's tongue
become speechless through emotion

On the tip of one's tongue
all but remembered

Rough end of one's tongue
sharp rebuke

Sharp-tongued
roughly spoken remark

Slip of the tongue
accidental revelation

Tongue hanging out
    thoughts of delicious food

Tongue-in-cheek
    ironic comment

Tongue-lashing
    scolding

Tongue-twister
    difficult word or phrase to pronounce

Tongue-wagging
    gossip

Saying

You've got a tongue in your head – why don't you use it?
    (there are those who need prompting)

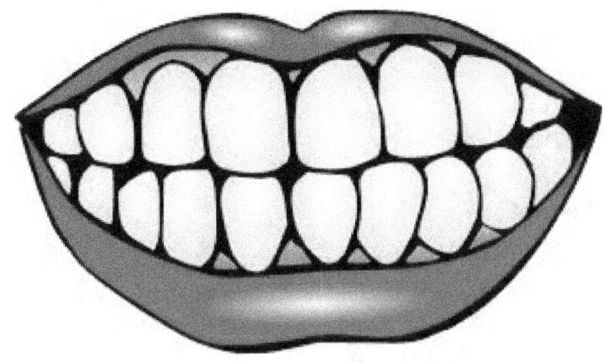

Armed to the teeth

Teeth

Armed to the teeth
> totally equipped

Bite off more than one can chew
> fail a commitment

Bite the bullet
> tackle an unpleasant task

Bite the dust
> abandon a project

By the skin of one's teeth
> by a very short margin

Cast (or fling) in someone's teeth
> taunt or reproach

Colt's teeth
> youthful excesses

Cut one's teeth on
    initial practice

Draw the teeth of
    make harmless

Fed up to the teeth
    despondent, have a grievance

Have teeth
    have adequate defence

In the teeth of
    against whatever obstacle

Kick in the teeth
    unjust blow

Lie through one's teeth
    do so brazenly

Long in the tooth
    advancing age (*analogy of the horse*)

Put the bite on
    extort money

Set one's teeth
    clench them

Set one's teeth on edge
    feel a disagreeable sensation in the mouth

Show one's teeth
    display aggression or apprehension

Stir dragons' teeth
    stir up trouble

Sow dragons' teeth
    stir up trouble

Stompers (*slang*)
    one's teeth

Sweet tooth
    a liking for sweet things

Take the bit between one's teeth
    purposeful

Teething trouble
    initial problems

Through clenched teeth
    stiffly, concentrating

Throw back in someone's teeth
    repeat what he said wrongly

Tooth and nail
    with vigour and determination

Toothless
    harmless

Toothsome
    delicious

Toothy (*toothy expression*)
    large pronounced teeth

What's biting you?
     why are you so angry?

With a fine-tooth comb
     thoroughly

Words thrown in one's teeth
     one's words rejected

Wrist

Slap on the wrist
     mild reprimand

Also available through Amazon